Garden Design For Everyone

Volume 2

Robin Johnson

Copyright © 2023 (Robin Johnson)
All rights reserved worldwide.

No part of the book may be copied or changed in any format, sold, or used in a way other than what is outlined in this book, under any circumstances, without the prior written permission of the publisher.

Publisher: Inspiring Publishers,
P.O. Box 159, Calwell, ACT Australia 2905
Email: publishaspg@gmail.com
http://www.inspiringpublishers.com

 A catalogue record for this book is available from the National Library of Australia

National Library of Australia The Prepublication Data Service

Author: Robin Johnson
Title: Garden Design for Everyone: Volume 2
Genre: Non-fiction

Paperback ISBN: 978-1-922792-83-9

Contents

Introduction..*v*
Preface..*xi*
Forward: Pictures of Australian native plants ....*xiii*

1. Getting Your Soil Right 1
2. The Design Process 14
3. Getting the Picture Right 30
   The Decorative Principle \ Flowering Plants 30
4. The Structural Principle 39
5. Garden Pathways 52
6. Living with a Hillside Garden 67
7. My Annual Rose chart 87

Appendix: Trees for our Gardens 91

Index 106

Introduction

Azaleas in full colour make a great entrance to a home or alongside a pathway

For the past 20 years both gardening and lifestyles have changed dramatically. This is primarly the reaon for my new book....

Garden Design For Everyone Volume 2

The natural world and suburban gardeners have learnt to adapt to changing conditions. Where we live has been affected by unpredictable weather conditions: e.g. extreme heat followed by cloud and torrential rain.

New housing suburbs have filled up hectares of precious farmland often by placing only one house on an entire block. In these circumstances, we need to understand how to use the highly prized small space left by developers to create a garden for a shady tree, or a space to grow a small garden.

Visiting gardens

To begin Volume 2, I recommend readers visit other people's gardens because this is where you can learn a great deal about developing your own garden and also receive useful ideas and - the best gift of all - inspiration!

Visiting enables you to learn how

- To create different moods in the garden
- To use hedges to create and divide different garden spaces
- To identify the variety of trees and plants that do well in your area
- To above all else see how different gardens work in your area

Volume 2 is dedicated to everyone who:

- Wants to learn more about improving their garden soils, and making garden compost.
- Wants to understand more about garden design processes, such as how to build a garden's structure particularly the soil.
- Has an admiration for roses and will see a benefit from a yearly planner.
- Is interested in an historical time line of garden design.

Introduction

At the conclusion of 'The Gardener Through History' I posed a question. What is in store for our future gardens and garden design?

To begin to answer this question, let me say that I believe a garden that hasn't been thoughtfully designed and planted is just a collection of plants. That is why Volume 2 explains through pictures and diagrams the principles and practice of simple garden design to suit our needs and nurture our environment in an ever-dwindling rural landscape.

> "to make a garden is to organize the established elements and add fresh ones, but the first principle of garden design one must be able to absorb all that we see the sky, the soil and the colour of the grass and the shape and nature of the trees" Russell Page, Education of a Gardener 1994 'page 45 Chapter 1.

In the future I hope gardeners will have the knowledge to plan and design a garden rarely seen before. I envisage domestic garden design will focus on native plants from local areas and planted in large quantities which brings a total natural look to the garden. This is what landscape designers call the mass planting effect, it brings a decorative style to your garden.

Gardens will need to be designed and planted to create shade areas appropriate for high summer temperatures and they will need to have soak- aways too, for periods of heavy rainfall.

Gardeners will need the knowledge to build their own water storage systems, above or below ground level.

I wrote in 2005 "private gardens will continue to play a vital role in reflecting the individual aspirations of the owners, providing essential ingredients crucial to their life". Today your garden will help to establish a heathy work-life balance, and it will continue to be a welcome place to escape from the hustle and bustle of the modern world.

Garden Design for Everyone Volume 2 continues the journey of how to design, develop and manage a garden in the modern era.

I explain in Chapter 5 the importance of building solid pathways as seen in these suburban gardens seen on the following pages.

Pavers are being embedded in landscaping gravel bordered by a brick edging.

Introduction

Seen in these two pictures a brick edging makes a solid pathway edging.

Gravel now laid on a finished pathway

Preface

In Garden Design for Everyone Volume 2, there are new chapters that appear with pictures and diagrams that validate many important principles and elements of garden design that a homeowner will face when developing a garden today. For example I have emphasised the importance of garden design principles such as

- balance and scale
- proportion
- decorative and structural design theories

Forward

Welcome to Volume 2 Garden Design for Everyone

To begin I want to share a selection of Australian native plants. Photographs are supplied by Ben & Ross Walcott, Red Hill, Canberra, these native plants are suited to plant in a cold climate landscape.

I have also included three plans to illustrate their planting in a garden setting.

Lomandra Hystrix. *Grevillea Lanigera*

Banksia media + copper *Acacia Howittii*

The golden wattle Acacia is a fabulous flowering tree, it creates a great display in any garden in a temperate climate.

Correa pulchella

Correa Decumbens

Correa Pulchella Pink

Correa Pulchella White

Forward

Boronia Heterhpulchepylla

Brachyscome Multiflora

'Dwarf Banksia' ideal for future gardens.

The Grass Trees are excellent for Australian woodland gardens ideal for mass planting.

As the name suggests, Grevillea 'Elegance' puts on a show. 2 metres in height spreading to 3 metres. They are hardy and easy to grow blooming for months of the year. The flowers are fragrant and spider-like, toothbrush-style, or large and brush- like 'growing to 3 metes.

Following are two plans for a native garden

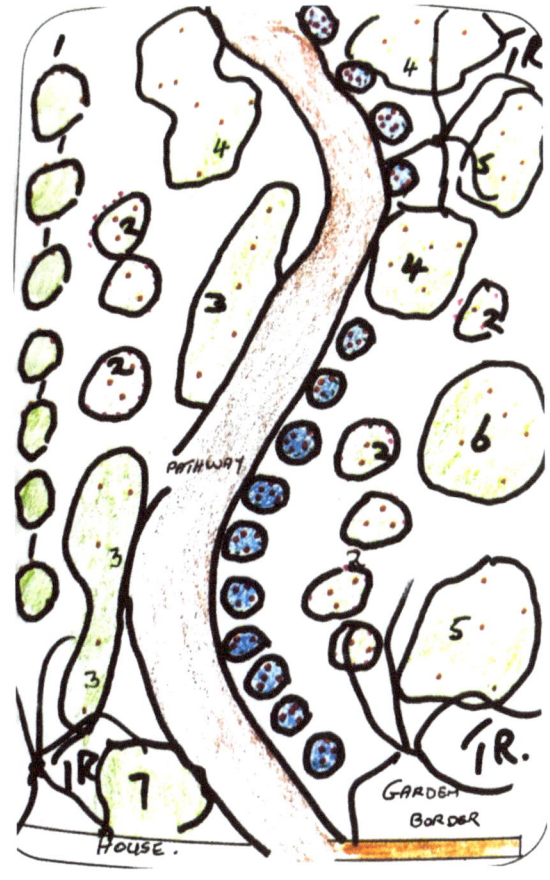

planting key

Pathway edging: brachycome multiflora

1. Banksia species
2. Lomandra hystrix
3. Boronia heterphylla
4. Correa Glabra
5. Correa pulchella pink
6. Grevillea lanigera
7. Correa Decumbens

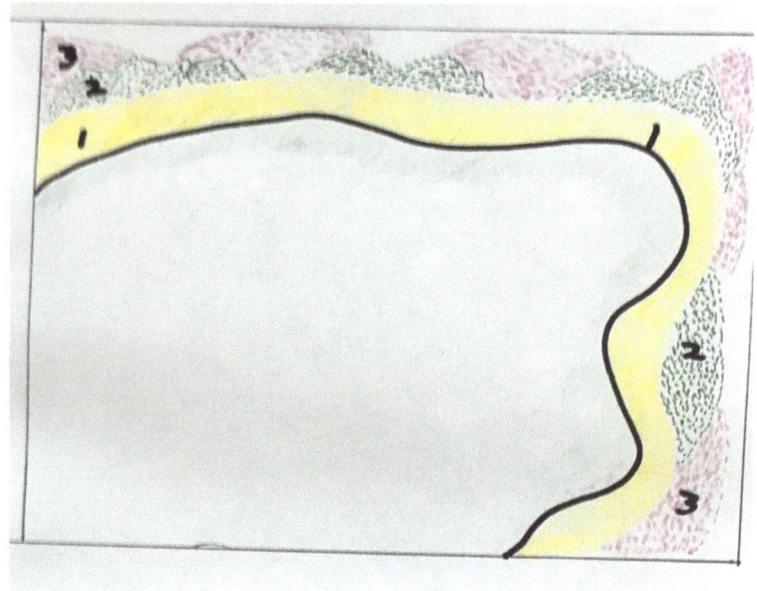

Planting key.

1. Correa Pulchella Pink
2. Grevillea Langera
3. Correa Pulchella

Chapter 1
Getting Your Soil Right

"It is important for people to protect our soils, agriculture and the environment because the collapse of soil leads to the collapse of human culture, civilization, livelihood and health.

However, soil resources have been overexploited in modern society and are currently on the verge of collapsing.. Soil is shown to be a living thing, a brief history of the relationship between soil and human health, cannot be underestimated".

Soil and humanity: Culture, civilization, livelihood and health, Katsuyuki Minami 2008

First word

To support the foundation of the garden we need to add organic matter during spring and autumn to the existing garden soil, this over time, will create a rich organic soil and add more depth thus enabling micro -organisms to live.

This chapter describes

- The creation of a garden compost, (I refer to it as the garden's engine room.)
- The value of general mulch (a soil protector) in the garden
- Examples of eucalyptus based mulches
- How to create a good depth of garden soil

1. Home compost

Making compost is one of the most satisfying garden projects. To create a successful compost a constant supply of raw and diverse material is needed. One household and garden will only be able to make a small compost pile of its own.

For example regarding my own compost pile, I am able to make 3-4cubic metres of compost every six months, this includes neighbours organic matter such as lawn clippings, hedge clippings and kitchen scraps.

The compost area

- Needs to be turned regularly, the compost is turned with a fork and watered which enables living organisms to enter the compost faster.
- Must be in the sunshine this ensures natural micro-organisms enter the compost to assist the breakdown of the raw organic material.
- Improves your garden's soil with a healthy compost frequently supplying the garden.

How do we know when the compost is ready?

1. It will show its progress by displaying large collections of worms, and micro - organisms.
2. A good compost will have plenty of diverse material(green and brown materials), it will heat up with a steady stream of heat given off as the compost is turned.
3. When the compost cools it is normally garden ready with all material becoming unrecognisable (including kitchen scraps).
4. At this stage, extra turning and sorting out of the compost material with a garden fork is still necessary, after which the compost will be ' garden ready'.

Making a good compost

Summary

The key for success is a steady amount of diverse green and brown material such as:

- Lawn clippings
- Autumn Leaves
- Miscellaneous garden waste, (however do not use grasses with running roots such as couch grass, or paspalum)
- Occasionally add blood and bone and lime

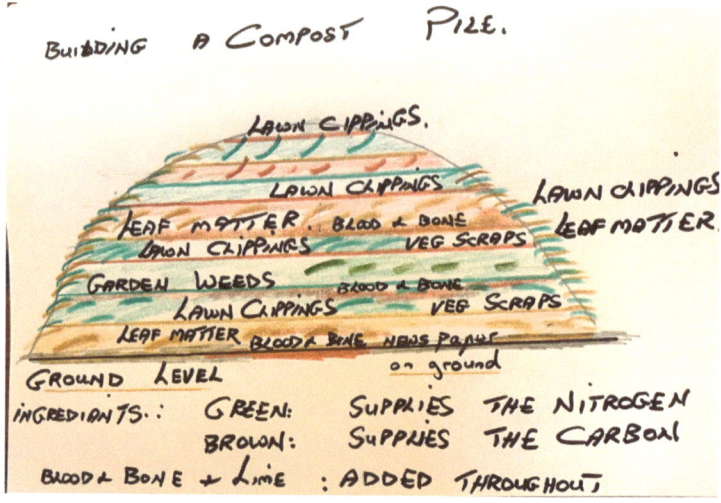

Illustrates a cross section building a home compost

1:2-1:5 These 5 pictures illustrate different stages of the breakdown and development of a garden compost.

The compost begins with a supply of raw leaves and other organic matter. In the Autumn, leaf matter makes a great start to a garden compost as it breaks down so quickly.

These 4 pictures show different stages of the breakdown and development of a garden compost. A compost will begin with the supply of raw leaves and other organic matter.

A wheelbarrow now ready with home compost

2. Building the foundation 'a mounded garden'

The advantages of a mounded garden:

- It allows more rainfall and natural seepage to soak into the garden, this will raise the water table which is vital in times of drought, and in turn allows the soil to hold more moisture and improves drainage.
- Creating a "natural hill and valley system" throughout your garden adds extra interest.
- Use garden soil available from a soil yard, mixed with garden compost.

A hill and valley mounded soil system built on virgin ground will create a successful planting area.

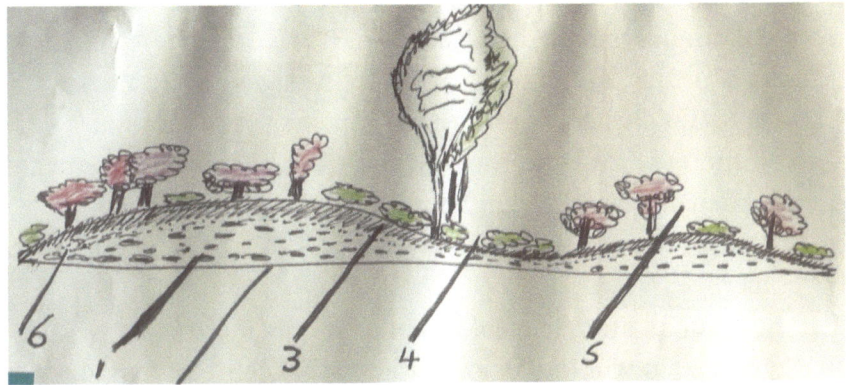

Diagram of a hill and valley mounded garden

Key:

1. Clean fill supporting existing ground soil
2. After planting mulch is spread throughout the surface of the mound.
3. Planting of ground covers and shrubs
4. After planting to finish off, add approximately 20 cms of a good garden mulch.

To Summarise :

Step by step to a mounded garden:

1. The mounded garden can be built any size and any shape throughout the garden, however it must be the correct proportion to look right in relation to the remainder of the garden.
2. Use soil yard fill to lay on the virgin ground.
3. Finally build up the mound with mushroom compost and garden soil and compost.

4. They provide an excellent foundation to the garden, and will create depth and height to the rest of the garden.
5. They need to be built to the correct scale to the remainder of the garden normally between 1.8m to 2.4m wide, this then allows the mound to taper down to its edges.
6. Mass plant ground covers on the top of the soil mound.
7. Soil mounds give the roots of the trees and shrubs room to establish and draw water from the extra soil.
8. In hot summers the soil mounds will keep the plant roots cooler.
9. The garden's drainage will be considerably increased.
10. Your garden will look a lot better, with a sense of height, and width.

3. Organic soils and composts: top dressing a garden

An organic mulch is a soil protector, protecting the soil from extremes of sunlight and rainfall. This is why it is added to the top of the garden soil, it is available in two forms:

1. Mulches that enrich and build up the soil.
2. Mulches that serve only as a soil protector.

Enriching Mulches are listed below they are all available in bulk from landscape supplies for the home gardener.

- Meadow hay
- Mushroom compost
- Pea straw
- Sugar cane
- Rice hulls
- Lucerne hay

Organic Mulches will:

- Improve soil depth and quality will quite quickly encourage earthworm activity over time.
- They will break down to form part of the top soil.
- Assist in controlling garden weeds.
- Add moisture and keep the plants roots system cool.
- Assist in the soil drainage.
- Ensure the whole landscaped area has a professional look.

Mulches that serve only as a soil protector

Eucalyptus Mulch is a by-product of the timber industry. It is a fine, shredded mulch, and is suitable for a vast range of garden types. It is light in colour, long lasting and attractive.

Eucalyptus Mulch is used for

- weed suppression,
- water retention
- soil improvement

NOTE: if using a red gum, or Eucalyptus Mulch or hardwood chip over an extended period of time, the garden will need regular Ph testing* (see note) to ensure the plants have the correct level of fertilizer application.

---

*Ph testing: it's important to follow directions: take samples of soil, they show, with an application of liquid and powder through a series of soil colours the availability of plant nutrients to the plant.

Horticultural grade Pine Bark.

Red Gum Mulch an attractive mulch used for a decorative surface of garden areas

Acknowledgements:

I would like to thank the landscape supply company TUNKS of Katoomba New South Wales.

They allowed me free access of their landscape yard for the pictures in this chapter.

In the soil yard ready for collection bulk soils and mushroom compost

Chapter 1 Summary .....

1. I reinforced how important it is for everyone to protect their soils, their agriculture and the environment, for the sake of our modern civilization, livelihood and health.
2. I emphasised the importance of buying soil either in bulk or by the bag for adding soil to your garden.
3. I gave reasons for building soil mounds in a garden, to create a natural hill and valley system.
4. I underpinned how important organic mulches and composts are when building mounded gardens.

Chapter 2

The Design Process

Chapter contents

- The design process of planning a garden
- The importance of climate and site
- Garden styles
- Understanding your garden's scale and proportion
- Beginning your garden picture
- Designing and maintaining a sloping garden

First word

Creating the right plan

I taught Adult Education in Canberra in the 1990's, home owners bought along their garden plans and ideas, I referred to them as their basic principles or 'getting an idea off the ground'.

We discussed the concept of 'time versus money' students learned their best design for their garden. However they didn't have the time to do the practical work, this is when I brought in landscape contractors to work with their ideas.

With my assistance they drew their garden plans, and hired the contractor to do the work, or just the earth works.

Note: Remember there are many computer garden design programmes available that would assist you with developing plans for your garden.

For the past few years, Australia has been in the grip of some extreme weather events, caused by La Nina and El Nino weather patterns, droughts being followed by extreme rainfall events.

1. Planning and developing your garden

In Garden Design for Everyone 2005 I asked the key question.

'What do I want from the space around my home and how do we know what kind of garden will suit our needs?'

In 2023 this continues to be the important question, below are some answers.

1. A well-planned garden continues to be your home's best asset, and will compliment the surrounding natural environment.
2. In the beginning it is imperative that a plan is drawn on paper, showing where your significant trees and shrubs will be planted, this will create your garden's foundation.
3. Planting trees and shrubs without a plan will result with just a collection of plants.

Getting the picture right 'The principles of planting'

- These include a structural element and a decorative element.
- Gardens can be either a mix of native or non- native plants.

Russell Page Education of a Gardener 1994 page 45 Chapter 1 in search of style wrote

> "We must draw a very clear distinction between style and decoration. I could consider no modern garden even remotely interesting as a work of art unless it could stand as such, be stripped of every single decorative attribute. A garden artist will only use the decoration to heighten its style."

Climate and site

Understanding the movement of the earth from summer to winter

In summer

In Australia the temperate climates are in the ACT, Eastern Victoria, and South Eastern New South Wales.

Note: It is always best to purchase a home that faces North, with only a few windows that face West, There will be no harsh westerly sun in summer coming into the home.

In winter the north facing rooms will receive warmth from the low sun in the north.

In winter

In Australia the winter sun of June, July and August, rises low in north east, and moves in a low arc and sets in the north western sky.

On a sloping garden Terraces and Pathways help establish scale.

A narrow path transvers around between two garden levels, eventually ending up with steps.

It is vital on a sloping garden that all the gardens are made to the correct proportion in relation to the slope.

Terraces seen here fit together to the right proportion to form unity to the natural landscape and are in harmony with the natural bush land.

The sloping gardens are planted with Rhododendrons and assorted evergreens to reflect the garden's proportion.

Understanding Scale and Proportion

'The basic essentials'

To begin your design these 3 drawings illustrate **how scale and proportion will affect the planning of your garden.**

Scale and Proportion are decisive in garden design, as they refer to the size of all objects in relation to each other.

Diagram 1 "Scale and Proportion"

A large scale

A normal scale planting

A small scale

The design process

The beginning of your plan

A garden's wish list is an excellent place to begin planning your garden.

Begin with a blank sheet of paper, and begin to draw a basic plan, (Plan 1) of what you want from your garden space, as the picture below shows.

What is it I want from my garden ?
What is it I need from my garden ?

They may include:
- An outdoor living place,
- Drying areas,
- Water tanks,
- Grass and hard surfaces,
- Sheds,
- Shade areas.

The Design Process

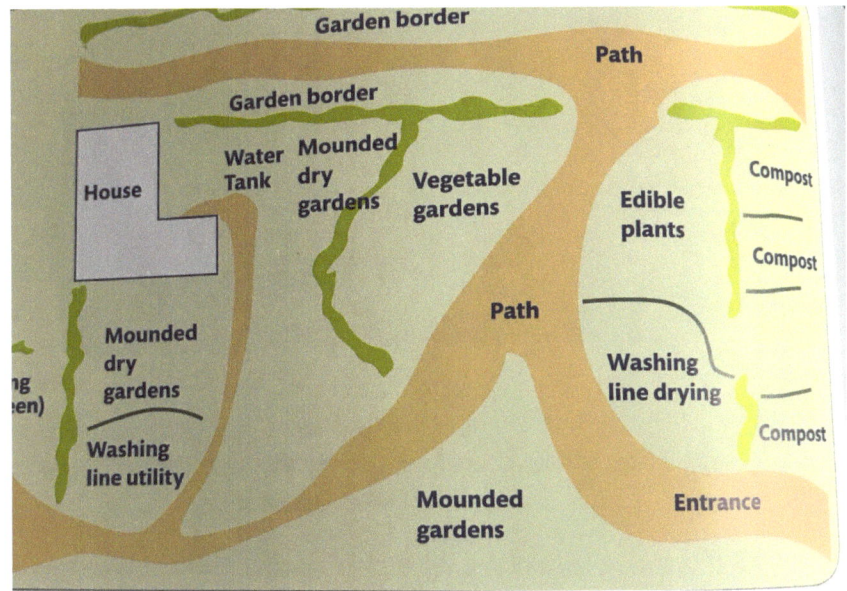

Diagram 3 (plan 1)

Understanding Style will begin with:

1. Dividing your garden space:

Start with having some basic principles in mind, and learn how to divide your garden to create the garden spaces you want.

Generally in any type of garden it will be the pathway that will symbolise your style.

A pathway too, will assist in creating the 'kind of garden you want' and what kind of garden is best on the site.

Understanding how to develop this style is paramount to the success of your garden.

The garden's pathways

Circular, or curved pathways represents an informal garden, whereas a straight pathway signifies a formal garden.

Whatever design you choose, pathways must go somewhere and have a purpose.

With a view of large cold climate conifers, we see gardens planted with evergreens around a fence line.

A large open garden as such as this has the capacity to be divided into several styles, formal and informal by including small hedges, and pathways or structures that help create separate areas.

Formal or informal Plan

Garden diagrams

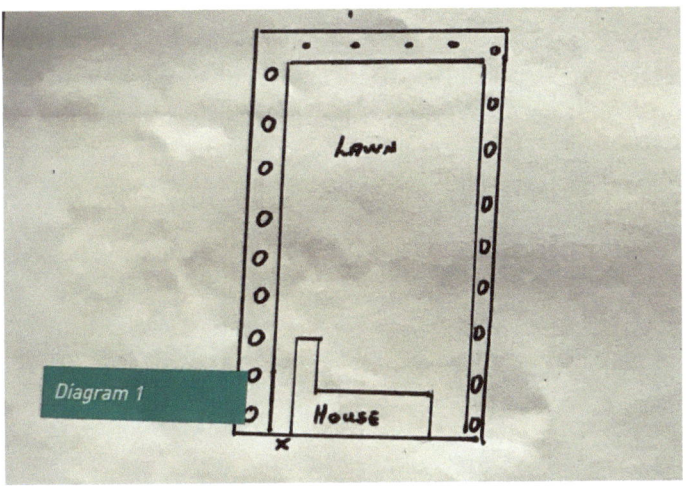

Often we see gardens such as this with planting around a fence perimeter

These plans continue to look formal, because of their coloured straight lines. Without any plants in design with an addition of various coloured circles, it becomes a more interesting plan.

The informal garden

Curved lines create the informal and interesting garden.

This plan converts from a simple, straight lined garden bed system often made "around the fence line, in front of an outside pergola" into an more interesting curved garden.

Note: This plan first appeared in Garden Design For Everyone Volume 1 2005

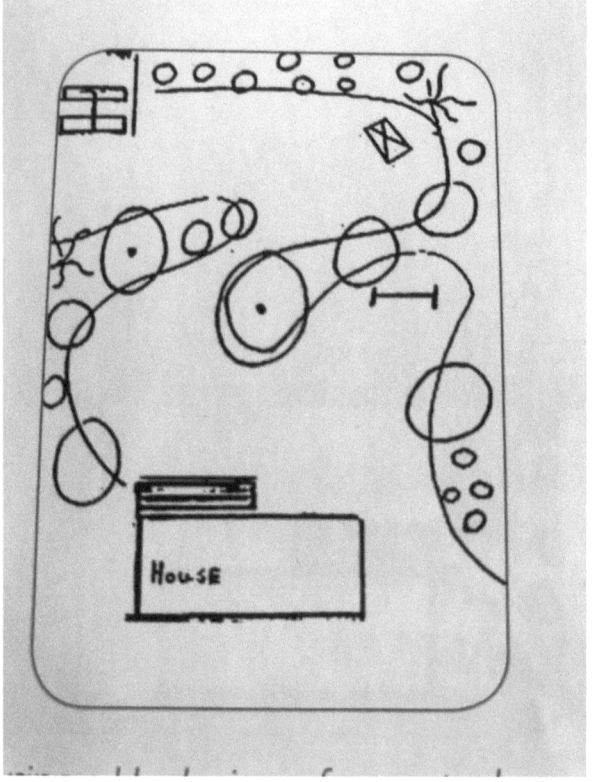

Note: In chapter 3, I emphasise the importance of the structural and decorative plants.

Planting plan for a garden in a cold climate, for spring interest.

1. lavender species
2. Spirea (May Bush)
3. Golden Diosma
4. Pittosporum Silver Song
5. Pittosporum James Stirling
6. Ornamental upright evergreen
7. Port wine Magnolia
8. Climbers
9. Perennials planted every two to three years.

FT 1 Prunus species Flowering Cherry
FT 2 Maple species Crab Apple
FT3 Standard prunus species

A garden border using 3 plants

- Using only three plants can make an interesting border

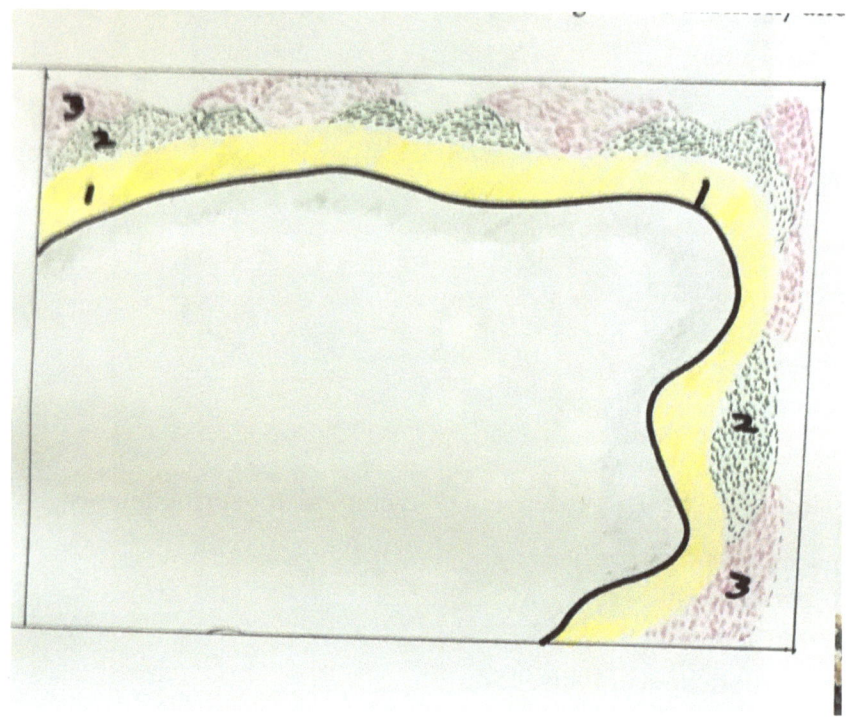

Plant list :

Three plants to create a blue garden.

1. Catmint Nepeda
2. Lamb's Ears Stachys Byzantina
3. Perennial stock

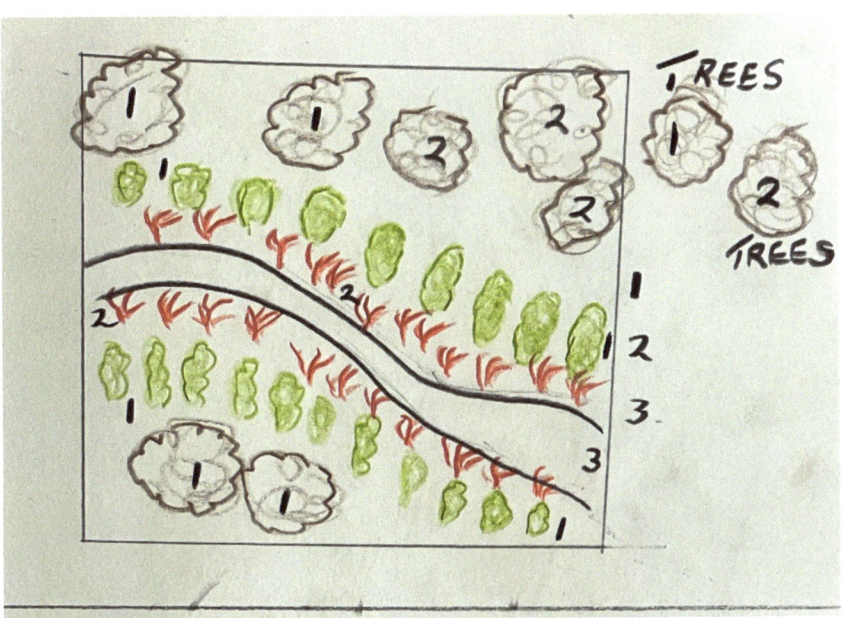

Key

A Border with 2 plants along a pathway and 2 spring flowering trees.
1. Bergenia Cordifolia (winter flowering, low growing perennial)
2. Blue grass, (Festuca Glauca)
3. Solid gravel pathway

Trees
1. Flowering cherry, Prunus Kanzan
2. Flowering dark leafed Plum, Prunus Nigra

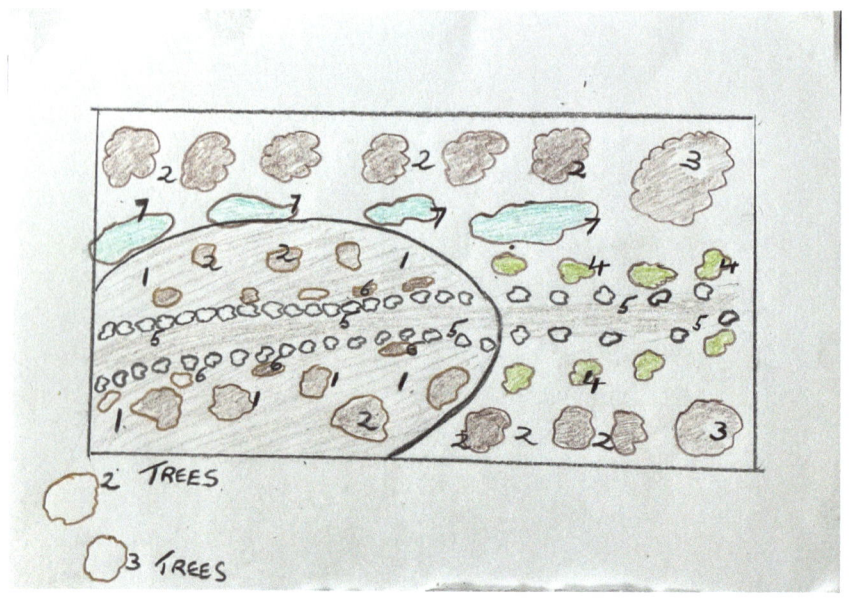

A cold climate (sunny) native garden using 6 plants.

Key

Trees

3 Eucalyptus Scoparia (White gum)

Plants
1. Correa alba, alongside pathway.
2. Melalucea spp /Eriostemen myoporoides (long leafed waxflower)
3. Correa Decumbens
4. Pathway edge
5. Native plants: ground cover
6. Correa Reflexa

Chapter summary

In this chapter I discussed the garden design process.

With a series of diagrams and pictures I reinforced the importance of the 'principles of planting.'

I also discussed

- How to begin your design, understanding garden style.
- I introduced 4 garden diagrams, with different planting strategies.
- Through three pictures the importance of understanding Scale and Proportion and how it affects the planning of the garden.
- I illustrated how Scale and Proportion is vital particularly on a sloping garden.

Chapter 3

Getting the Picture Right

The decorative principle
Flowering plants

This chapter describes:

- My thoughts of how to create colour with flowering plants.
- An understanding of the garden's 'decorative principle' and how it can be used throughout the year.

The Decorative Principle

The Annual and Perennial plants

Having discussed structural plantings in the previous chapter (trees and hedges), we now move onto the garden's colour which I call the 'decorative principle'.

I have seen many clients over the years, showing them how to design a colourful garden throughout the year. It boils down to how your favourite plants are arranged to create patterns. Their purpose is to bring unity and colour to the garden, as I have shown in the following pictures they bring balance to your structural plants. Their effect can be maximised by planting them in groups of single colour.

Mass planting

In cold climates Polyanthus, (pictured) Pansies and Violas, flower through autumn/ winter, whilst Petunias and Salvia are ideal for flowering through summer.

Polyanthus creates a terrific 'mass display' on urban street

Summer annuals such as Zinnia's and Red Salvia, Red Tulip make ideal mass displays for large pots.

Snow in Summer (Alyssum Tomentosum) seen here massed around a large rock.

Snow in Summer (Alyssum Tomentosum) here as an edging.

Flower circles of Polyanthus, Impatiens, Petunias make tremendous displays throughout spring and summer.

A rose garden 'massed display'

Roses too are ideally suited for mass planting, both single or multi colour themes.

Note in chapter 6 I have included a Rose Calendar.

'For a theme of some kind a basic idea is essential. It will set the rhythm of the whole garden, down to the smallest details.' Russel Page (1999)

Roses make a fine decorative contribution

A large rose garden displaying a single colour.

The garden's theme

A Garden theme can be expressed in various ways particularly:

- By growing garden's trees to provide height, and spring or autumn colour, and interest.
- By having your evergreen small, non-flowering, hedging shrubs meandering through the garden.
- With flowering shrubs, that come into flower throughout the seasons.

- By planting bird-attracting Australian native shrubs, such as Grevillea, Hakea, or non-native shrubs such as Lavender, (Lavandula) or Rosemary (Rosmarinus).
- By planting single colour rose gardens, full of your favourite colour rose.
  (Author's note this is my favourite way of displaying a rose garden)
- By mass planting together annuals or perennials.

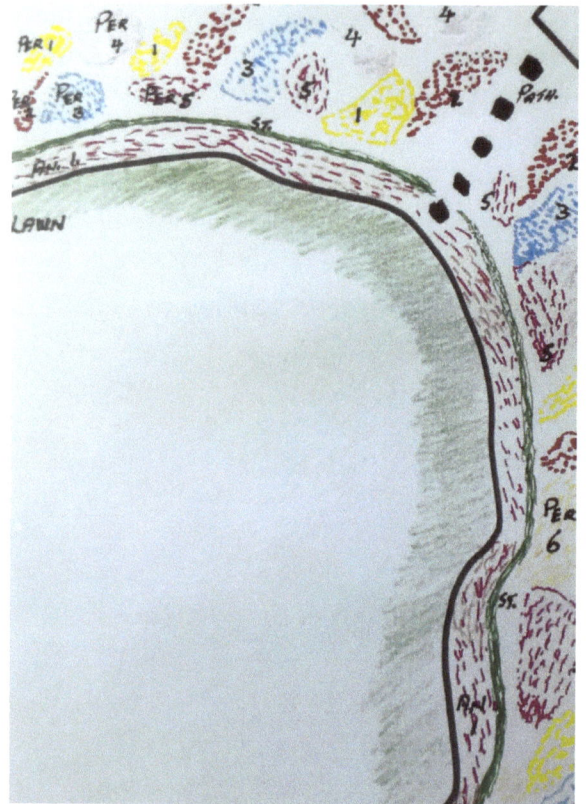

*A colour plan illustrating a decorative edge,
running against a lawn approximately 10x10 metres*

Key :

1. Small conifer
   spring \summer focus:
2. Sea side Daisy (Erigeron)
3. Autumn Crocus clumps
4. Penstemons
5. Standard roses
6. Box hedging

Annuals: Pansy edging to lawn \ for autumn-winter
Green edging (on plan) Small : Mondo grass
Note : Your garden's theme will depend on the ideas you choose.

Colour through- out the year

Seasonal annuals planted on the garden edge maximise the garden's decoration. This too will enhance the garden's pattern within the structural evergreens, in this plan the structural evergreen is Mondo Grass.

I want to emphasise the benefit of a permanent 25cms outside border on a shrub or perennial garden. It creates a permanent edge in which to plant colour (annuals) throughout the year.

Through-out the year a walk into any garden centre will see an array of annual or perennial flowers in punnets, or small pots. They will all be suitable to provide colour in the corridor, next to the lawn.

In a large suburban garden Azaleas too make a fine spring display.

Chapter summary:

- Planning is the answer to creating seasonal colour in your garden.
- This will take understanding and experience, particularly using the plants you like.
- Remember it will be how you arrange your colourful plants that will provide colour for your garden borders throughout the year

To provide seasonal colour here are my recommendations:

1. Annual plants for a cold climate
Late Winter- early spring: Pansies and Violas.
Summer: Zinnia, Petunia, Marigolds.

11. Perennial plants

Easter daisy, Aster
Penstemons
Japanese windflower

My special mention

Bulbs, Rhizomes
Iris, Daffodils, Tulips Autumn Crocus

Chapter 4
The Structural Principal

1. Hedges

This chapter describes why hedges:

- Create the garden's backbone
- Are the evergreens that define a garden border, or pathway
- Can be used to open and close garden space and to create different garden rooms
- Can be used to complement your decorative flowering plants

Hedges large or small are the garden's major '*element of structure*' they bring balance to your garden.

A little History

As early humans (Stone Age, Bronze Age), (*reference: The Gardener Through History Robin Johnson*) began to settle and form communities all across Britain, they made enclosures from plants they had collected and planted from British hedgerows. Plants such hawthorn, blackberry, privet, beech, hornbeam, yew, English box, oak were used as fortifications for safety to keep out marauding native tribes and wild animals.

From the Middle Ages to Modern times, Britain's farm fields have been a collection of hedgerows, often using layered hedges. Hedges continue to provide shelter for wildlife and divide farm fields to grow modern arable crops.

Hedge layering

Hedge layering is a skill, both an art and a science, it is as common today as it was in the middle ages.

From the early Middle Ages, British farms were defined by the layered hedge using native British plants.

Today a walk through Britain's laneways and countryside, one will still see many fields separated and defined by layered hedging.

Layering incorporates specific tree species, and is still practiced all over England and Europe. In these pictures deciduous European beech *Fagus sylvatica*, is made into a serpentine hedge. This creates an interesting hedge even in winter with its reddish foliage. *Note this is a highly skilled profession that creates this layered effect.*

Hedges are the beginning of the structural plan.

Start with drawing a simple hedge design, maybe like this one, it includes a hedge and evergreen shrubs.

This simple garden plan validates planting a hedge along a path using evergreens such as, Sasanqua Camellia or Lavender

In a cold climate small conifers, box hedges (Buxus) or lavender (lavendula) are ideal evergreens to validate a garden's small structural planting.

This plan shows different coloured circles, that can be interpreted with different evergreens.

The circles bring together the principles of good garden design, bringing together a balance of structural and decortive principles.

Box hedging (Buxus Sempervirens) seen here creates a special circular garden.

Planting plan
1. Seasonal annuals
2. Buxus Microphylla (box hedging)
3. Iris, + standard roses
4. Rosemary.

(Buxus Sempervirens) Box hedging here in an urban landscape

A lavender (lavendula x intermedia) hedge is created by close planting.

The Structural Principal

A low growing Pittosporum makes an ideal low hedge.

Although it still provides privacy and security from a golf course, a mixture of low evergreens provide a perfect alternative to a hedge.

Planting key of Evergreens include:
- Thuja species (left of gate)
- Myrtus right-hand corner
- Picea, species (right of gate)
- Dwarf picea in foreground
- Ceder (Cedrus Atlantica Glauca in golf course)

Pittosporum Tenuifolium Silver Song and James Stirling makes an ideal tall sculptured hedge. Pittosporums are great evergreens that lend themselves perfectly for hedging.

Most gardeners will prune this variety into tall hedges reaching 3- 5 metres.

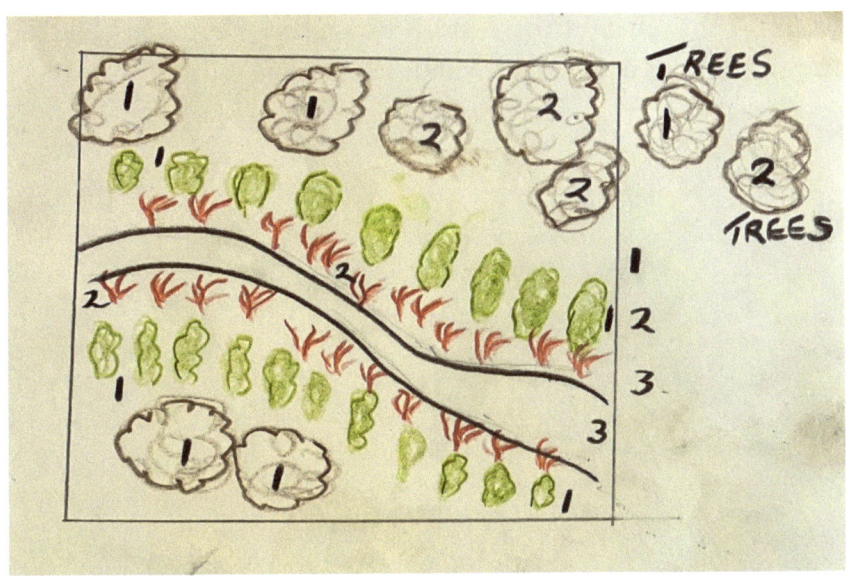

Key: Planting

1. Green : Box hedging(Buxus Fruiticosa or Sempervirens) a small hedge, planted approximately 400mm each side of a pathway, provides the garden's structural backbone.
2. Red: Seasonal annuals (for example: summer, Salvias and Petunias for Autumn - Winter Violas, Pansy planted to create the border for the pathway. They provide the garden's 'decorative backbone.

Trees
1. Flowering Cherry, Prunus Kanzan.
2. Manchurian Pear, Pyrus Ussuriensis.

To finish this chapter: here are 5 examples of suitable hedging evergreens for a cool climate suburban garden.

NO 1.

A tall vertical lifter is bought in for maintenance on this tall Lawsoniana conifer hedge

NO 2

Photinia 'Red Robin'

NO 3

NO 4

Camellia Sasanqua in cool climates not only lends itself to creating a great specimen, by adding autumn colour, it makes a stunning hedge. They are available in a large variety of colours.

NO 5.

Azaleas in cool climates make an ideal low hedge.

Low hedges make an ideal centre strip in an urban street

To end this chapter I want to recap on its importance.
- Hedges are vital to give your garden its backbone, and are the beginning of the structural plan.
- A well-designed garden is ultimately divided into two, using two design principles:
  1. The decorative principle
  2. The garden's structural principle like hedges, trees, pathways.
- When you begin your garden draw a plan to emphasise simple hedge designs, like the ones shown in this chapter.

Chapter 5

Garden Pathways

In my first book of Garden Design for Everyone I stated whatever garden style is decided, it's the pathway that will reflect its true style.

In volume 2, I reinforce this by dedicating a chapter to this scenario.

I have outlined my 10 ideas to create the ideal garden path:

- A path is another important structural element when building a garden, it becomes the major line of communication throughout the garden
- A path must have a purpose, nothing is so forlorn as a path leading to nowhere.
- In large gardens a path often circumnavigates the whole garden to end up back at the house.
- A path should lead from place to place as directly as possible, but it can also show off special garden features.
- A path will define your garden's style, either a formal or informal garden, and illustrates the garden's scale and proportion.
- A path divides your garden space and creates different moods, around the garden.
- Paths are often made using grass, using the width of a large lawn mower as a guide, often as wide as 2-3metres.
- Garden paths are simple to make, however their width is important, a couple lines of bricks, approximately 1600mm apart, with a solid base, or use paving slabs they too will create an ideal pathway.

1. Building a garden path

Use solid pavers and colourful gravel to make a good pathway. When building a garden path, it can be built either with soft or hard edges.

The hard gravel makes the path excellent for providing dry walking throughout each season, but particularly in winter the cold frosty mornings seen in the pictures below show a garden pathway built with the brick edgings and paving slabs laid on a gravel-bed.

Circular gardens with surrounding pathways reflect the scale and proportion of the whole garden.

The construction and development of a pathway

The following four pictures illustrate a household pathway construction, taking the correct scale and proportion, into account.

At the beginning of a pathway construction, to a correct scale, an excavator was hired to move soil.

A bobcat was hired to move soil to create the final shape of the pathway.

With its final shape in place, a brick edging is laid on both sides, with a base of metal dust in order to lay the paving slabs.

Notice the pathway's width is exactly in the right proportion to the width between the home and fence.

In the next 3 pictures a brick edging is laid to join an existing pathway before gravel is laid to show the different divisions of separate gardens. The correct scale and proportion is seen with the joining of both pathways being the same width.

This garden pathway now takes shape laying the brick edging.

The pathway's final outcome is now a garden centre-piece and is completed by adding the feature tree Crab Apple tree (Malus Ioensis).

A Pathway for a country garden

For a country garden, shady pathways covered with gravel and timber edging takes a visitor through its woodland. It's built to wind around Eucalyptus trees, and other shady areas.

Evergreens are planted throughout this woodland area include Rhododendrons, Viburnums and Azaleas, pine chip is laid on the ground under the Eucalyptus trees.

A country pathway

The following pictures are courtesy of Hillside Garden, Hartley Valley near Blackheath NSW.

This magnificent country garden, and its tremendous winding garden paths take visitors around the whole garden, through a feast of hardy perennials, flowering at different times of the year. Together with magnificent tall conifers and shade trees visitors have a stunning garden to visit. Superb shady sitting-out areas are present throughout the garden, taking in the outstanding views of the Kanimbla Valley.

Note: These pictures have been used with permission of the owners of Hillside Garden, Blackheath NSW.

Mixed ground covers grow over solid paths, make good walking.

Snow in Summer (Alyssum) makes a good pathway edge.

Pathway Plans

Example: 1 A Pathway plan
for a cold climate.

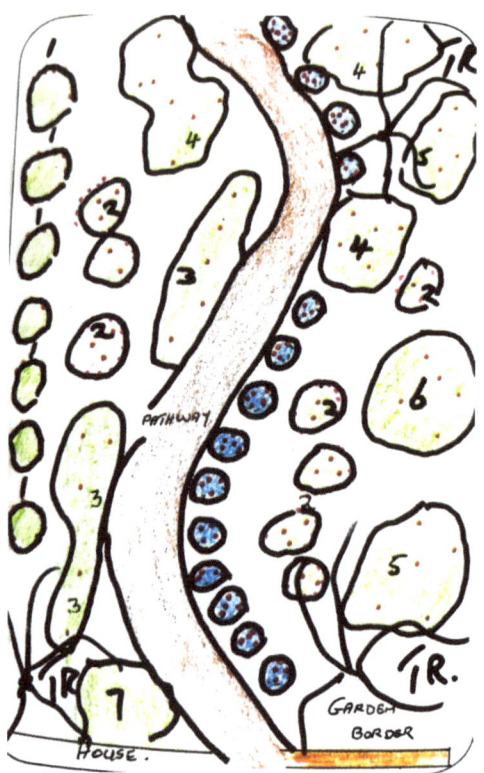

Planting key for a cold climate garden

1. Pittosporum hedging species
2. Coleonema Spp. The Golden Diosma
3. Lavender spp
4. Special deciduous shrubs for Spring flowering.
5. Evergreen conifer
6. Evergreen hardy shrubs such as Escallonia
7. Lavender

Along the pathway is a mixture of annual and perennial plants, featuring 2 flowering cherries

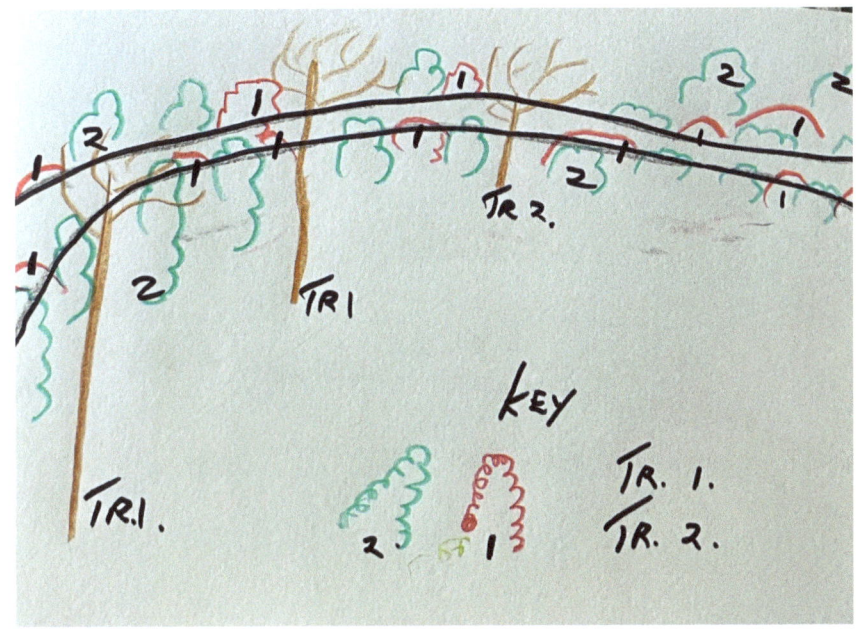

Plan 2

Another planting key for a garden in a cold climate.

Tr 1 Tree 1: large weeping cherry

Tr 2 Tree 2 Gleditsia (honey locust)

Evergreen 1 Buxus Sempervirens English box

Evergreen 2 Azalea species

Plan 3 pathway plan

1. Evergreen azaleas

Trees

2. Prunus species, flowering cherries

3. Malus Floribunda Crab Apple

1. Callistemon 'Harkness'
2. Callistemon sieberi
3. Carex species
4. Dianella longifolia
5. Correa decumbers x reflexa
6. Callistemon 'Hannah Ray'
7. Acacia spectabilis
8. Leptosporum Pink Cascade
9. Lomandra filiformis
10. Melaleuca incana dwarf
11. Banksia spinulosa
12. Correa decumbens (alongside path)
13. Correa alba (alongside path) hedge

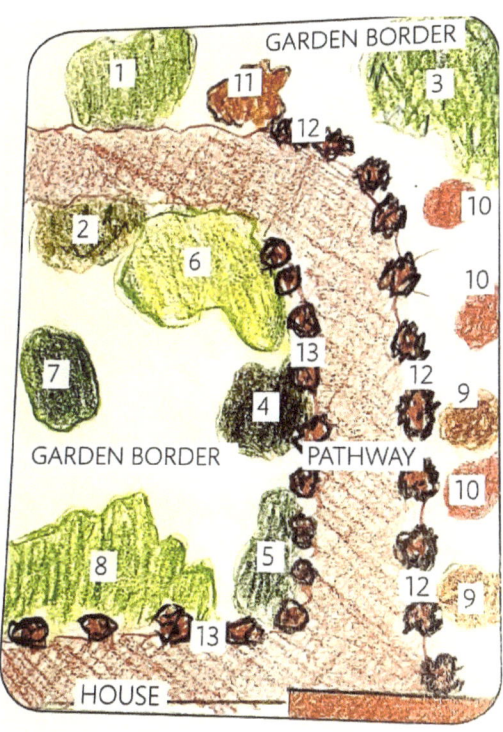

Chapter summary:

- Most importantly when constructing your garden pathways my advice is keep your ideas simple.
- I discussed with a series of illustrations how garden pathways will effect the division of space and the garden's scale and proportion.
- The decorative and structural garden elements can be enhanced with a pathway meandering through gardens or natural woodlands.
- I mentioned how garden pathways can be laid with grass, using the width of a large lawn mower as a guide.
- Garden paths are best made of solid materials, such as paving slabs, crushed granite, or quartz, and are often seen with concrete edges.

Chapter 6

Living with a Hillside Garden

Many homeowners buy or own a property built on a hillside, with a sloping garden either to a road or native bushland. The area at either the front or back of the home will have a steep "slope away", often the answer is building retaining walls, or rock embankments, to save storm water and drainage problems.

When confronted with a hillside garden understanding scale and proportion is vital.

Nothing will look so out of place if your scale of plantings is out of proportion to the sloping garden.

Scale my definition This is the size of something in relation to something else.

This chapter:

- Is meant to meet the needs of a family designing a hillside garden.
- Together with a series of pictures explains why scale is paramount for the success of the garden.
- Illustrates with pictures how a series of steps and pathways are integral to the correct scale.
- Reinforces how critical it is to have good access to the hillside garden.
- Shows my selection of plants and hardy groundcovers suitable for a rocky or hillside garden.

To begin maintaining or constructing a hillside garden ask yourself several key questions:

- Through extended periods of rain, what is the drainage and water flow?
- How can we prevent soil erosion?
- Are the natural rocks that are in the hillside stable or do they need strengthening by adding further rocks placements?
- What are the local Australian native plants which do well in the local area?

Travel around your local area and list your own local Australian plants, for hillside planting.

This hillside property leads up to the neighbour's roadway to take in the scenic view. Its terraces progress down the hillside with the last terrace falling away to bushland.

A top lawn terrace landing, and points to remember

The width of the lawn terrace in relation to the height of this stone wall is important to the success of this hillside garden.

Winding pathways and terraced gardens at different levels, take the visitor through different areas of the hillside.

1. Steps

In all hillside gardens a series of steps, that provide safe and easy access, is going to be vital to the success of the garden.

I now illustrate the kinds of steps, and stepways, that can be built on a hillside garden.

1. The side way step
A "side way" step is often built at right- angles to dry stone -walls. This will soften the entrance or exit.

2. The straight step
The straight step down to a next terrace will define a hillside slope; it will accentuate how steep the slope is.

3. The step landing
When building steps if space allows use no more than five steps, before creating a step landing this will soften the slope, and create a better scale within the hillside.

Paul Sorenson worked as a landscaper and designer in the Blue Mountains. He was a master builder of dry-stone walls, and used this sideway step many times, as seen here in the left picture, in this Leura garden. He used this many times as an entrance to the next level of a terraced garden. The straight step with a landing he used where more space allowed.

2. The stepping pathway

These 8 pictures illustrate steps and stepping stones meandering up and down through a hillside garden. Railings are critical in helping maintain easy access. This too ensures safe passage from one level to the next. A contractor is seen trimming extensive evergreen shrubs.

Plants are illustrated Rosa Multiflora, Hebe, Juniperus Conferta, Coprosma, Coleonema (Golden Diosma).

2. Grass terracing

These 4 pictures illustrate how grass terracing can be used on a hillside garden.

- The steepness of the slope will determine the necessary terraces, and this effects the composition of the hillside.
- For gardens laid out on the terraces, it's always a good idea to have two or three ways one can return to the level space close to the house.

On hillside terraces sleepers are used on two levels to stabilise its gardens. Planting includes Rhododendrons, Tree ferns, Elephant Ears(Bergenia) Hebe, Hydrangea, all are ideal evergreens for a cold climate.

3. Hillside views

On the hillside we want to accentuate all the views. Several pictures below, illustrate the importance of the view from a hillside country garden.

View from the top of the hillside garden showing Mount Solitary in the Blue Mountains.

A view of the Kanimbla valley taken from Hillview garden, it has been designed to melt into the incredible surrounding landscape.

4. The board walk

A wooden slated board-walk at the bottom of the slope allows access to the natural bush-land for maintenance and for fire control.

Plants seen here include Ericas, Banksias, Callistemon (bottle brush) all are extremely hardy evergreens.

PART 2

Here is my short-list of plants for a rocky, temperate climate, hillside garden.

Ajuga Repens

Portulaca Oleracea this plant thrives in dry conditions.

Hebe Coleonema Diosma, Catmint Nepeda both extremely useful for planting on a hillside.

Golden Diosma

Bergenia Cordifolia a clump-forming hardy evergreen perennial suitable for hillside gardens.

Gaura (The butterfly bush) / Rosa multiflora are both extremely hardy and ideal for a hillside garden.

Hydrangea, Hebe, Coprosma, Erigeron, Alyssum, Snow in Summer they are all plant species excellent for a natural looking hillside garden preventing soil erosion. They create an intensive root system that holds the hillside soil in place.

My lists of Australian native and non-native ground covers and low-growing shrubs that I recommend for hillside planting.

1. List of native shrubs to one metre

Hillside planting		
Native shrubs	Variety	Cultivar\common name
Correa	Glabra	
Correa	Pulchella	
Astartea		
Baeckea		
Callistemon		Bottle brush
Grevillea	Reflexa x	Decumbens
Grevillea	Royal mantle	
Lomandra	Longifolia	Tanika
Melaeuca	Incana	
Grevillea		Gaudi Chaudi
Viola	Hederacea	Native violet
Grevillea		Royal Mantle

2. Non-native ground cover and small shrubs to I metre

Hillside planting	
Non native	common name
Portulacea	Pigface
Stipa aurundinacea	Golden Ornamental grass
Poa Sieberiana	Blue ornamental grass
Coleonema pulchrum	Green diosma
Coleonenma aurea	Golden diosma
Santolina	Cotton Lavender
Nepeda	Catmint
Stachys byzantine	Lambs ears
Rosa Inca	Wild rose
Thymus nitidus	Creeping thyme
Thymus Serpyllum	Creeping thyme
Ajuga reptans purpurea	

Plans illustrating the hillside garden

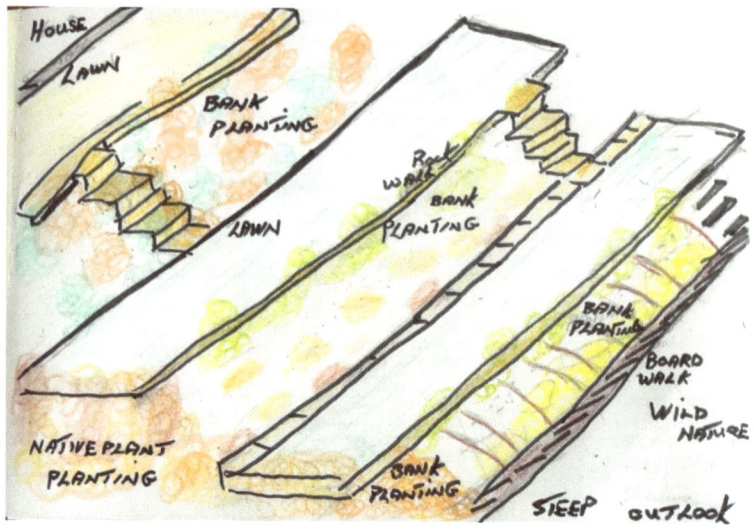

- A plan of a terraced garden, showing terraces with bank plantings.

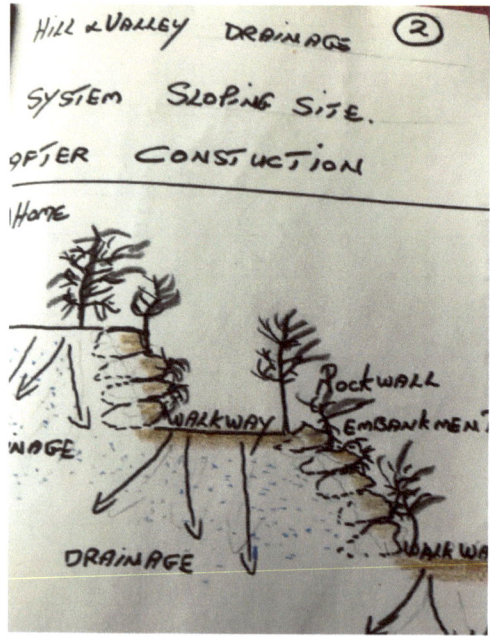

A side-look plan of a hillside garden.

PART 3

Drawings of rock placements

Illustrations of rock placements so they look part of the natural landscape. It is always advisable to draw a concept plan before going ahead with the work.

Placing the key rock is the trickiest piece of the art.

The key rock must face the same direction as it was in its original bush setting. The key rock in this picture below is the one closest to the tree. Then arrange randomly similar sized rocks around the key this will create a bush style rock feature.

Replicating how bush rocks look in nature, is in itself a work of art.

The dry river bed seen here in its natural setting.

Note: here large and small rocks, and pebbles have been used to create a dry river bed. Consistent arrangements have been avoided, such as placing rocks in a straight line or creating constant patterns.

Chapter 7
My Annual Rose Chart

To close Garden Design for Everyone Volume 2, I have included a pictorial look at a rose garden which I have titled My Annual Rose Chart.

January	February	March
Summer		Jobs Summer pruning begins in early January, trim stems down to 3-4 buds, and remove the flower dead heads.

Winter in the rose garden

Pruning begins in late July - August. In the cooler southern states of Australia this is also the time for planting bare root roses, as seen in the June picture how they arrive in our garden centres.

Rose gardens seen here are being prepared for winter pruning.

May	June	July
 		Winter Notes 

My Annual Rose Chart

August		September
		Pruning climbers along fences

October	November	December
Spring- Summer begin adding Rose Food to roses. Roses enter full flower.	Spring- summer	
Notes, Look out for black spot, I recommend an 'eco friendly fungicide spray for roses. Ensure that they are watered regularly.	NOTES: Continue adding Rose Food to roses	

Appendix

Trees for our Gardens

What do we mean by a Tree?

A tree is typically a single or multiple trunk, growing to over 4 metres in height. It has the the capacity to bear lateral branches, at some distance from the ground.

In the second volume the appendix is used to recommend suitable trees for a suburban garden, trees for shade, spring flowering or autumn foliage.

When it comes to choosing your trees bear in mind:

- How big will the tree grow, not just in the next 5 years, but in the next 25 years?
- Are we growing the tree for shade, for autumn or spring interest?
- How far will the tree's roots grow and canopy spread?
- Are they being planted to create a windbreak?
- Are we planting trees to create shady areas for shade loving plants such as Azaleas, and Camellias?
- What Autumn colour or Spring flowers will the trees provide?
- Are the trees suitable for planting in small groups?
- Will they provide shelter for wildlife?

The right tree for the right spot

A common problem is that you might have inherited a garden with the wrong tree in the wrong place, and wonder just what do we do with it.

Of course there are generally two options

1. Remove the tree,
2. Use the existing tree(s) to fit into your new garden,

Spring interest trees.

In gardens in cool temperate regions spring is the season, blossom trees come alive, they are often the first to burst into flower, with their white, pink, or red flowers.

Four of my favourite blossom trees are:

- The flowering Cherry (Prunus species)
- Crab apples (Malus species)
- Prunus Elvins
- Dark leafed Plum (Prunus Nigra)

I wrote in Volume 1, that planting trees in small groups, is the key to success; in particularly flowering trees such as the flowering Cherry Prunus Kanzan.

I recommend this strategy again in Garden Design for Everyone Volume 2.

Following are pictures of

1. Blossom trees
2. Weeping trees for the garden

Prunus Kanzan is a superb medium growing flowering cherry suitable for a cold climate. In the distance is a white flowering cherry. This cherry will grow approximately 6 metres wide, and 4 metres high.

Prunus Elvins is an ideal small flowering tree, illustrated here grouping together they give a strong sense of garden structure and style.

The flower plum (Prunus Nigra) makes a fabulous medium sized flowering tree.

2. Weeping trees

Prunus Subhirtella (Weeping Cherry)

Prunus Subhirtella (Weeping Cherry)

Nursery stock Weeping Cherry

Crepe Myrtle

3. Autumn colour Trees- The Maples

The Maples are a large group of trees that are divided into two groups the Palmatum and Dissectum. They make up some of the finest trees for small and partly shady gardens.

All Maples have magnificent Autumn colour, of reds, yellows and oranges, becoming brighter in the cooler weather.

Acer Dissectum

Acer Palmatum, grown as an archway in Robin Johnson's garden

The Maples make a fine collection of autumn colour (Acer Dissectum and Acer Palmatum)

4. The Silver Birch - Betula Alba

Silver birch: Betula Alba

The Golden is Faxinus excelsior aurea a valuable medium growing garden tree, with yellow bark and bright yellow foliage in autumn.

Metasequoa this conifer makes a terrific large lawn feature tree.

THE PLANS

Plans 1

Trees for Spring Colour

Organising your deciduous trees on a suburban block

key

1. Weeping tree
   weeping Birch, Betula\ weeping flowering cherry or, Prunus Subhirtella, winter flowering cherry Pendula
2. Prunus Elvins (small group)
3. The Betula Alba; Silver Birch (small group)

Plan 2

Trees for Spring interest

Plan 2 key

1. Dark leafed plum Prunus Nigra
2. A group of Prunus kanzan
3. Golden Ash Fraxinus Aurea
4. Weeping feature trees, such as Weeping Birch, (Betula pendula) or Weeping Cherry Prunus (Subhirtella Pendula)

Plan 3

Plan 3

Evergreen Conifer in a large country estate

Finally

- All year, round trees give the garden it's height and interest.
- Trees assist with soil and water retention and shelter for bird life. Their roots provide the soil with its stability, and prevent soil erosion.
- Trees through the process of photosynthesis take in carbon dioxide and give out oxygen into the air we breathe.
- Trees transpire water taken up from their roots to their leaves, through the transpiration stream.

The transpiration stream is the plant's capacity to evaporate water through its leaves that has been taken up from its roots.

Index

A

Ajuga Repens 77
Alyssum 32, 61, 80
annuals 31, 35, 37, 43, 47
Author's note 35
autumn 1, 30, 34, 36, 49, 91, 99, 101
Azaleas v, 37, 50, 58, 91

B

backbone 39, 47, 51
Banksia xiii, xv, xvii
beech 39, 40
Ben & Ross Walcott xiii
Bergenia 27, 74, 79
blackberry 39
black spot 90
Blue Mountains 71, 75
board walk 76
borders 38
Boronia xv, xvii
Box hedging 36, 42, 44, 47
British hedgerows 39

C

Calendar 33
Callistemon 76, 81
Camellia 41, 49
Catmint 26, 78, 81
climate xiii, 14, 22, 25, 28, 38, 41, 48, 62, 63, 74, 77, 93
colour v, vii, 9, 30, 33, 34, 35, 36, 37, 38, 49, 91, 98, 99
compost vi, 2, 3, 4, 5, 6, 7, 8, 12
conifer 36, 48, 62, 101
conifers 22, 41, 60
Correa xiv, xvii, xviii, 28, 81
crushed granite 66

D

deciduous 40, 62, 102
decorative principle 30, 51
design vi, vii, viii, xi, 14, 19, 20, 22, 23, 29, 30, 41, 42, 51
diagrams vii, xi, 23, 29

E

environment vii, 1, 13, 15

F

Flowering Cherry 25, , 27, 47, 92, 93, 102
flowers xvi, 37, 91, 92
foliage 40, 91, 101
future gardens vii, xv

G

garden design vi, vii, xi, 14, 19, 29, 42
Garden Design for Everyone 2005 15
garden fork 3
garden's backbone 39
garden style 29, 52
Garden styles 14
Garden theme 34
Gaura (The butterfly bush) 79
Getting the picture right 15
Golden Diosma 25, 62, 73, 78
gravel viii, 27, 53, 57, 58
Grevillea xiii, xvi, xvii, xviii, 35, 81

H

hedges vi, 22, 30, 39, 40, 41, 46, 51
hill and valley 6, 7, 13
Hillside iii, 59, 60, 67, 75, 81
Horticultural 10
Hydrangea 74, 80

INDEX

I

Impatiens 33
informal 22, 23, 24, 52

L

Lambs ears 81
landscaping viii
lavender 25, 41, 44
lawn 2, 36, 37, 52, 66, 69, 101
Lawsoniana 48
layering 40
Lomandra xiii, xvii, 81

M

Maples 98, 99
Marigolds 38
Melalucea 28
moods vi, 52
mulch 2, 7, 8, 9, 11
Myrtus 45

N

native iii, vii, xiii, xvii, 15, 28, 35, 39, 40, 67, 68, 81
New South Wales 11, 16
Non-native 81
north facing 16

O

oak 39
organic 1, 2, 4, 5, 8, 13

P

pathways viii, 22, 51, 54, 57, 58, 66, 67, 70
patterns 15, 30, 85
Paul Sorenson 71
Perennials 25
Petunia 38
Photinia 48
Ph testing 9
Pine Bark 10
Pittosporum 25, 45, 46, 62
planning 14, 19, 20, 29
Planning 15, 38
Plans 62, 82, 102
planting vii, xiii, xvi, xvii, 7, 15, 19, 23, 29, 30, 33, 35, 41, 44, 63, 68, 78, 81, 88, 91, 92
Polyanthus 30, 31, 33
Portulacea 81
Port wine Magnolia 25
proportion xi, 7, 14, 18, 19, 52, 54, 55, 56, 57, 66, 67
Prunus 25, 27, 47, 64, 92, 93, 94, 95, 96, 102, 103

R

Red Gum 11
rocks 68, 84, 85
Rosa Multiflora 73
roses vi, 36, 43, 88, 90
Roses 33, 90
Russell Page vii, 16

S

Salvia 30, 31
scale xi, 8, 14, 18, 19, 20, 52, 54, 55, 57, 66, 67, 70
Scale my definition 67
Sea side Daisy 36
shade vii, 60, 91
Shade 20
Sheds 20
shrubs 7, 8, 15, 34, 35, 41, 62, 72, 81
site 14, 16, 21
soil erosion 68, 80, 104
Soil mounds 8
soils vi, 1, 8, 12, 13
spring 1, 25, 27, 33, 34, 36, 37, 38, 91, 92
steps 18, 67, 70, 72
structure vi, 39, 94
styles 14, 22
suburban v, viii, 37, 48, 91, 102

Summary 3, 13
summer vii, 16, 30, 33, 36, 47, 90
Summer 31, 32, 38, 61, 80, 87, 90
sun 16, 17

T

terraces 68, 74, 82
The Gardener Through History vii, 39
theme 33, 34, 36
themes 33
Trees iii, xvi, 27, 28, 47, 64, 91, 98, 102, 103, 104
Tulips 38
Tunks 11

V

vertical lifter 48
Visiting gardens vi

W

water vii, 6, 8, 9, 67, 68, 104, 105
Water tanks 20
weeds 9
weeping cherry 63
winter 16, 17, 27, 30, 36, 40, 53, 88, 102